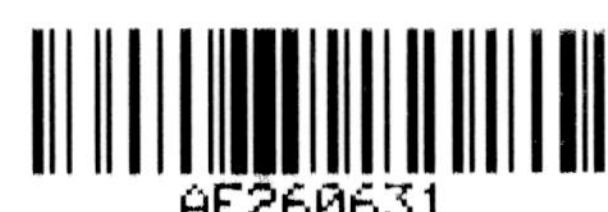

CHARACTER
colouring

illustrated by christian campbell

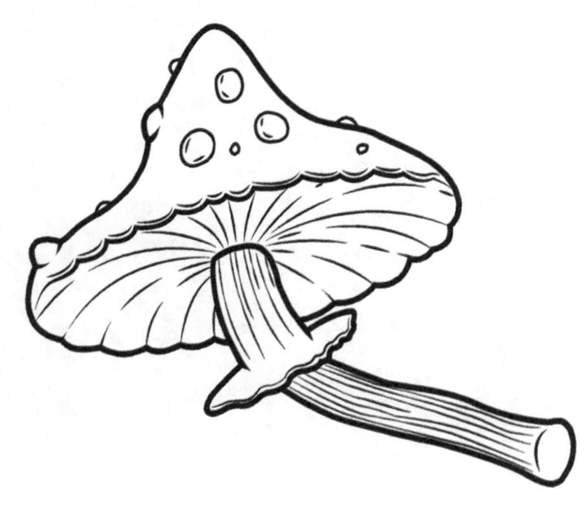

Contact : chriscampbellillustration@outlook.com
Instagram : chris25campbell

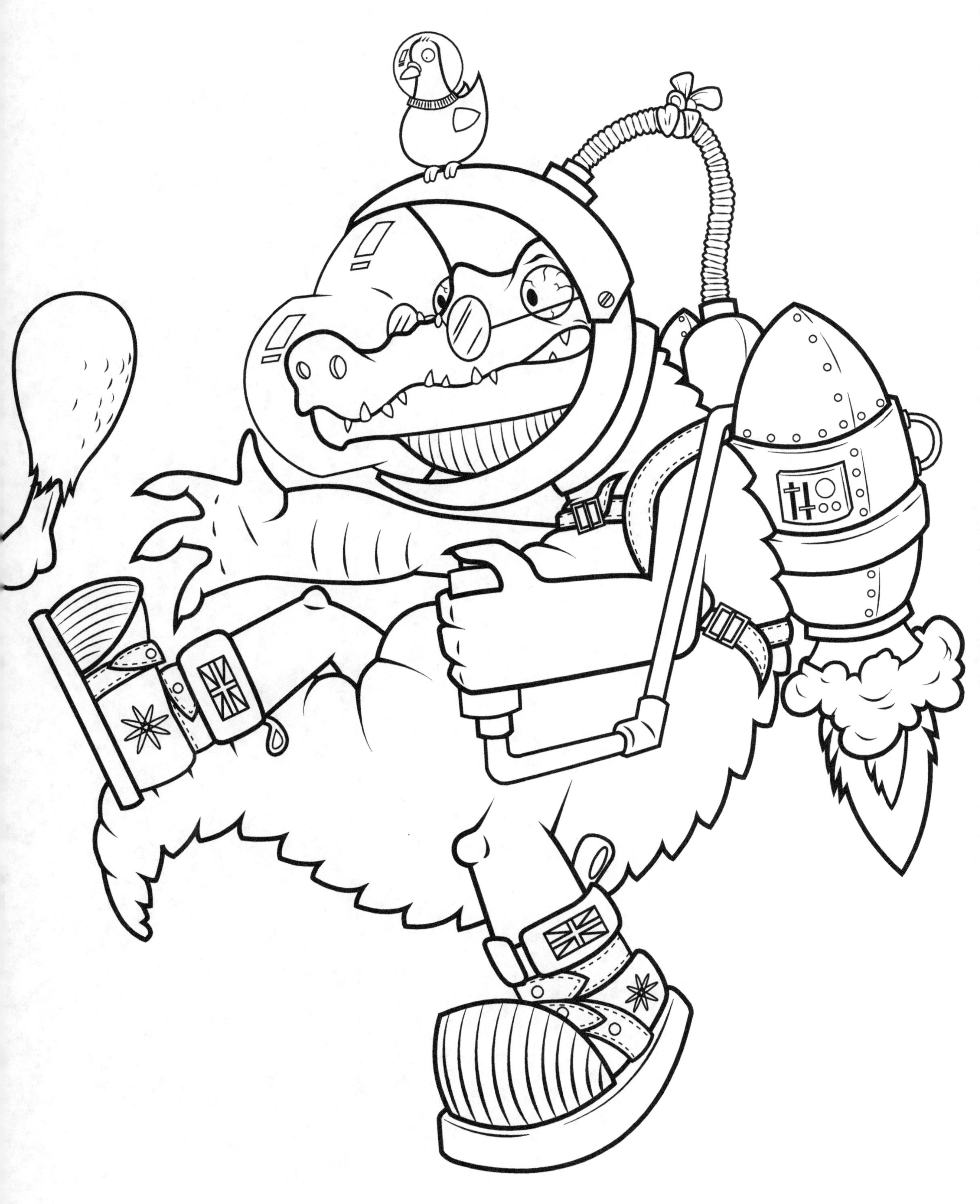

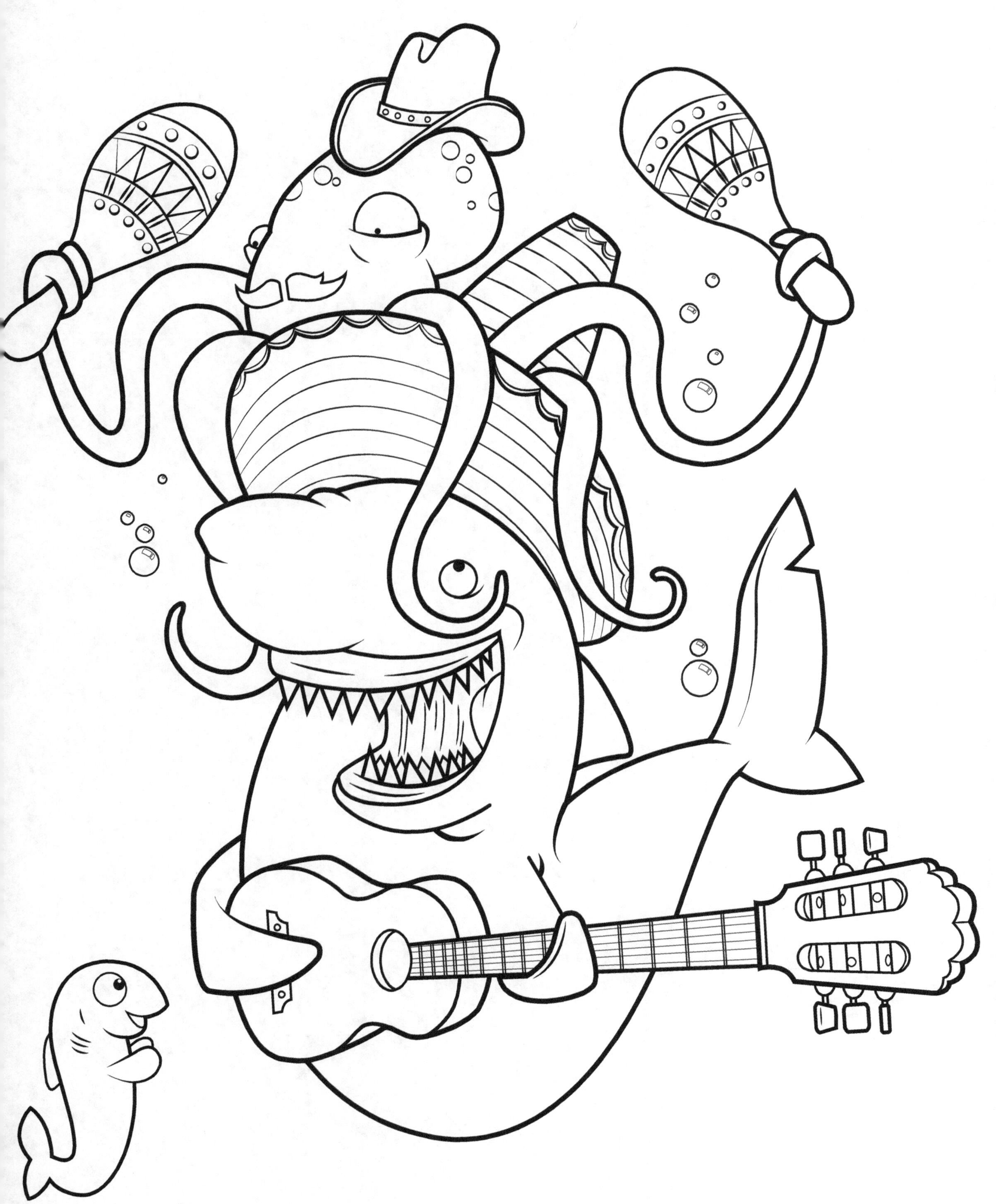

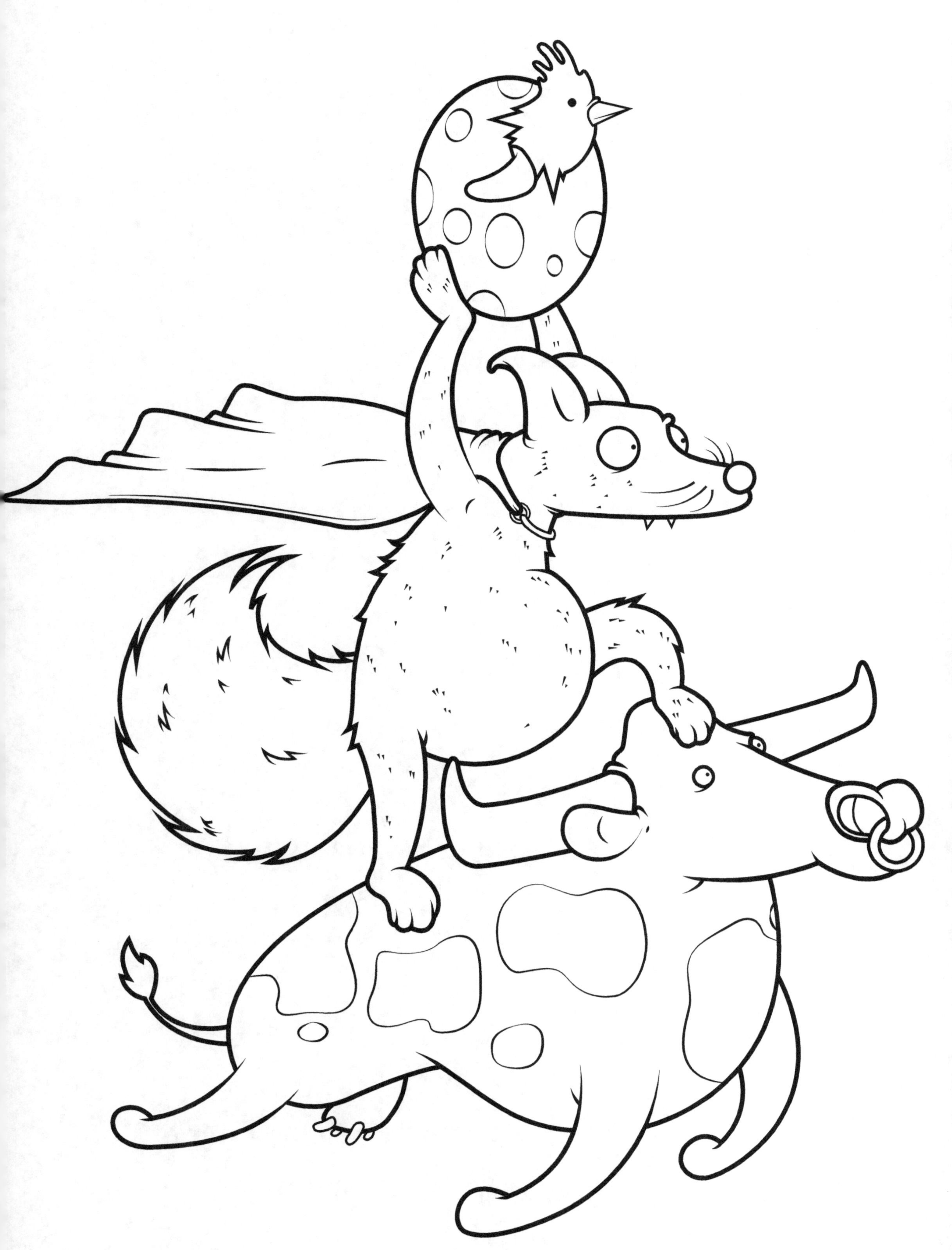

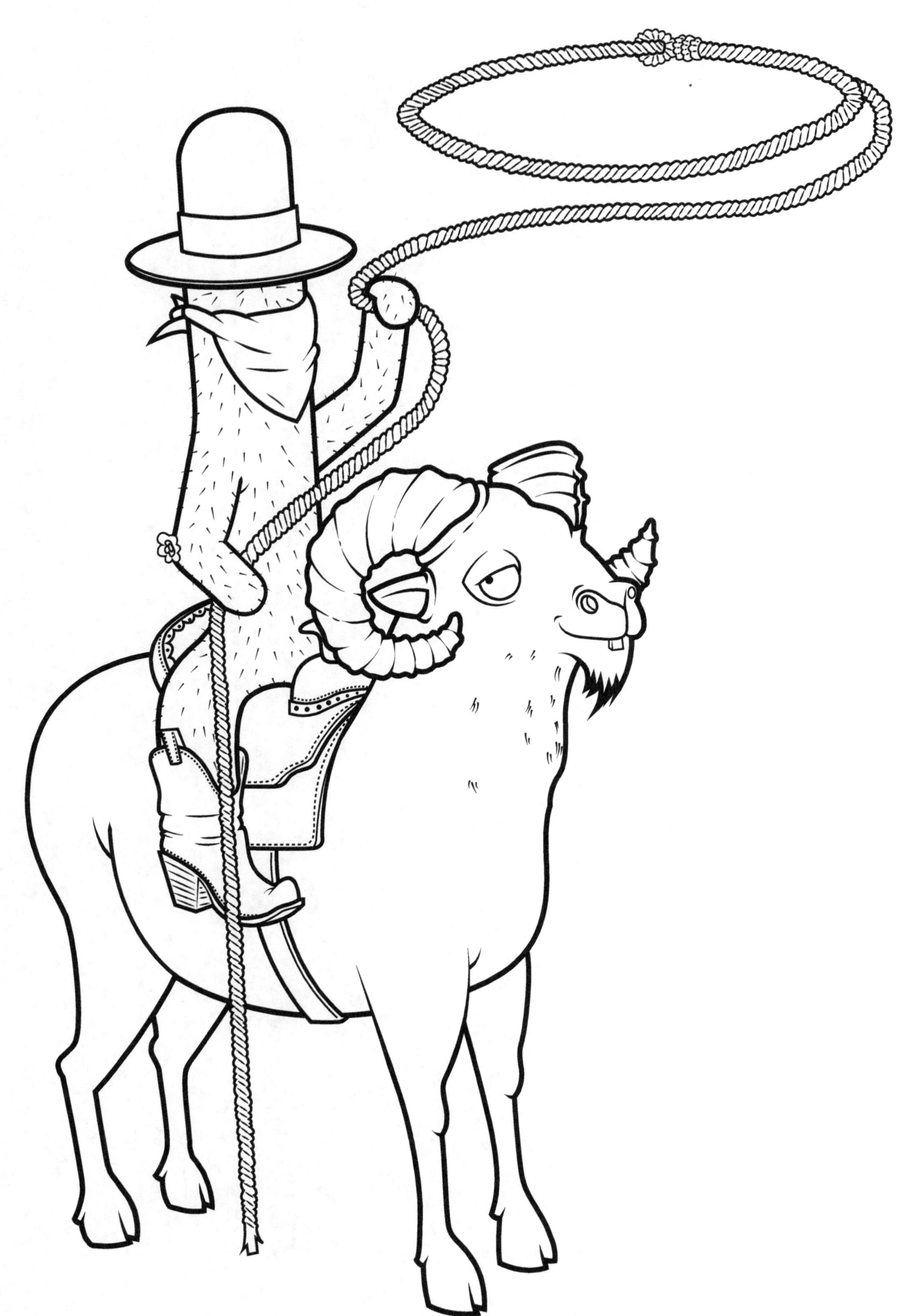

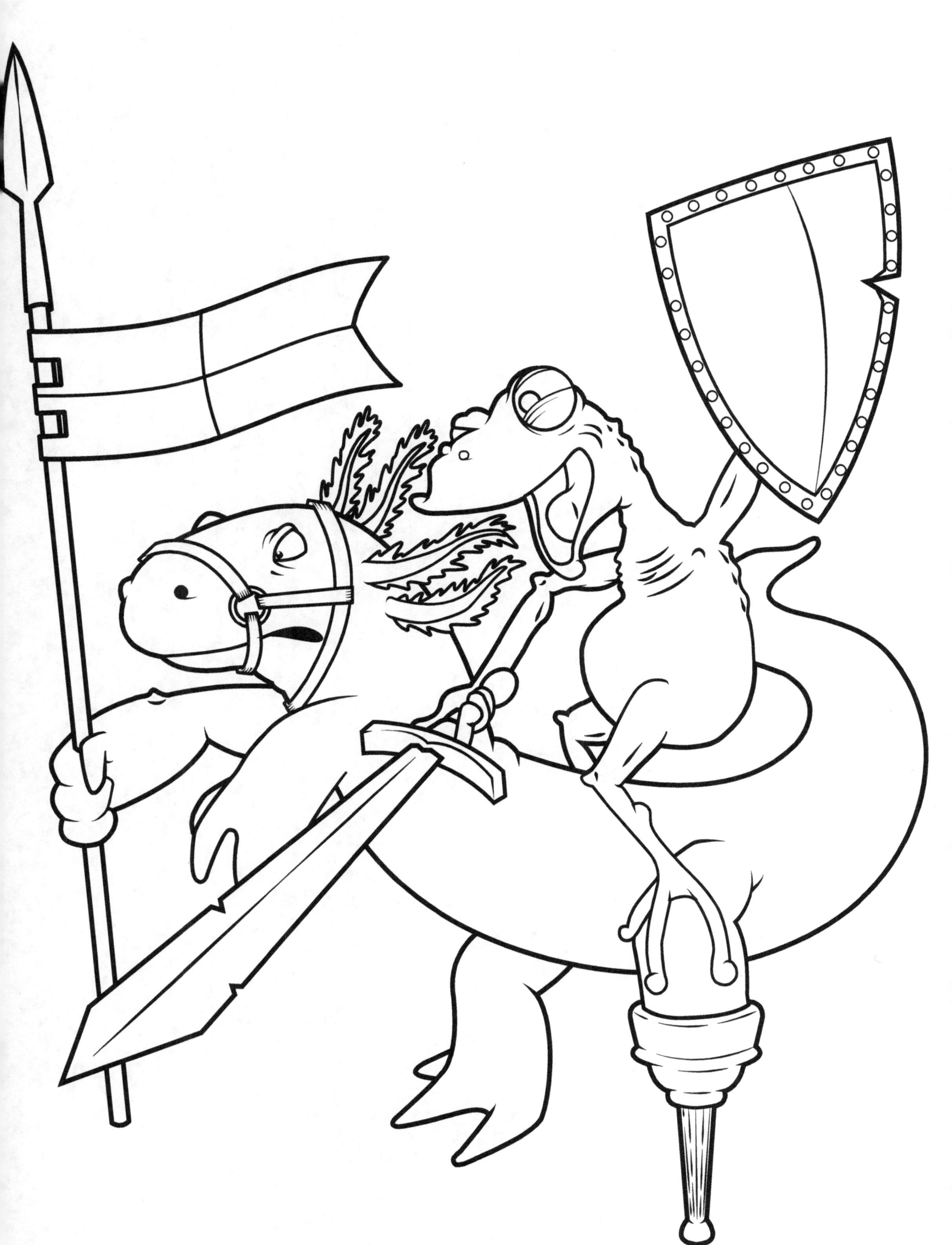

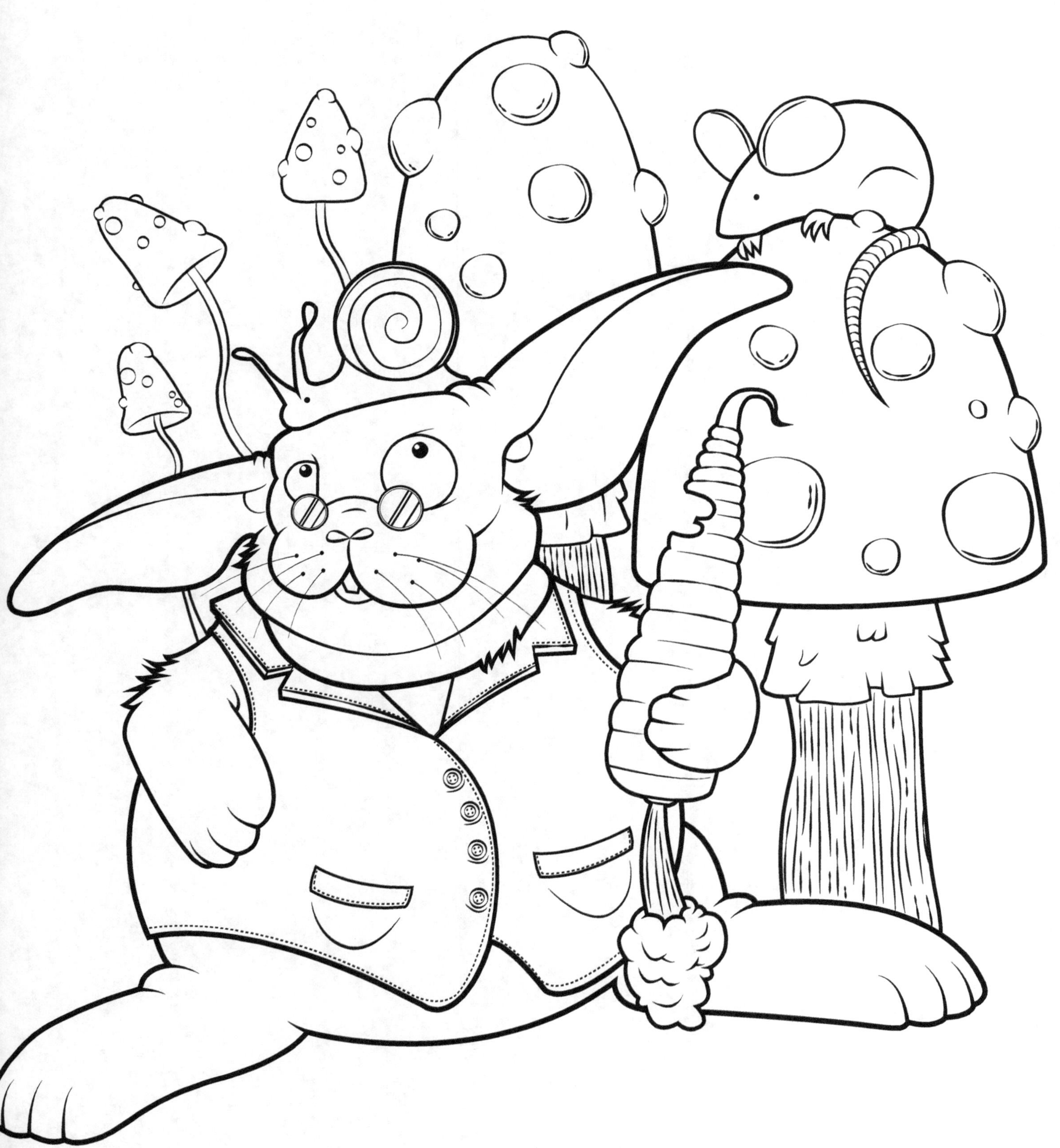

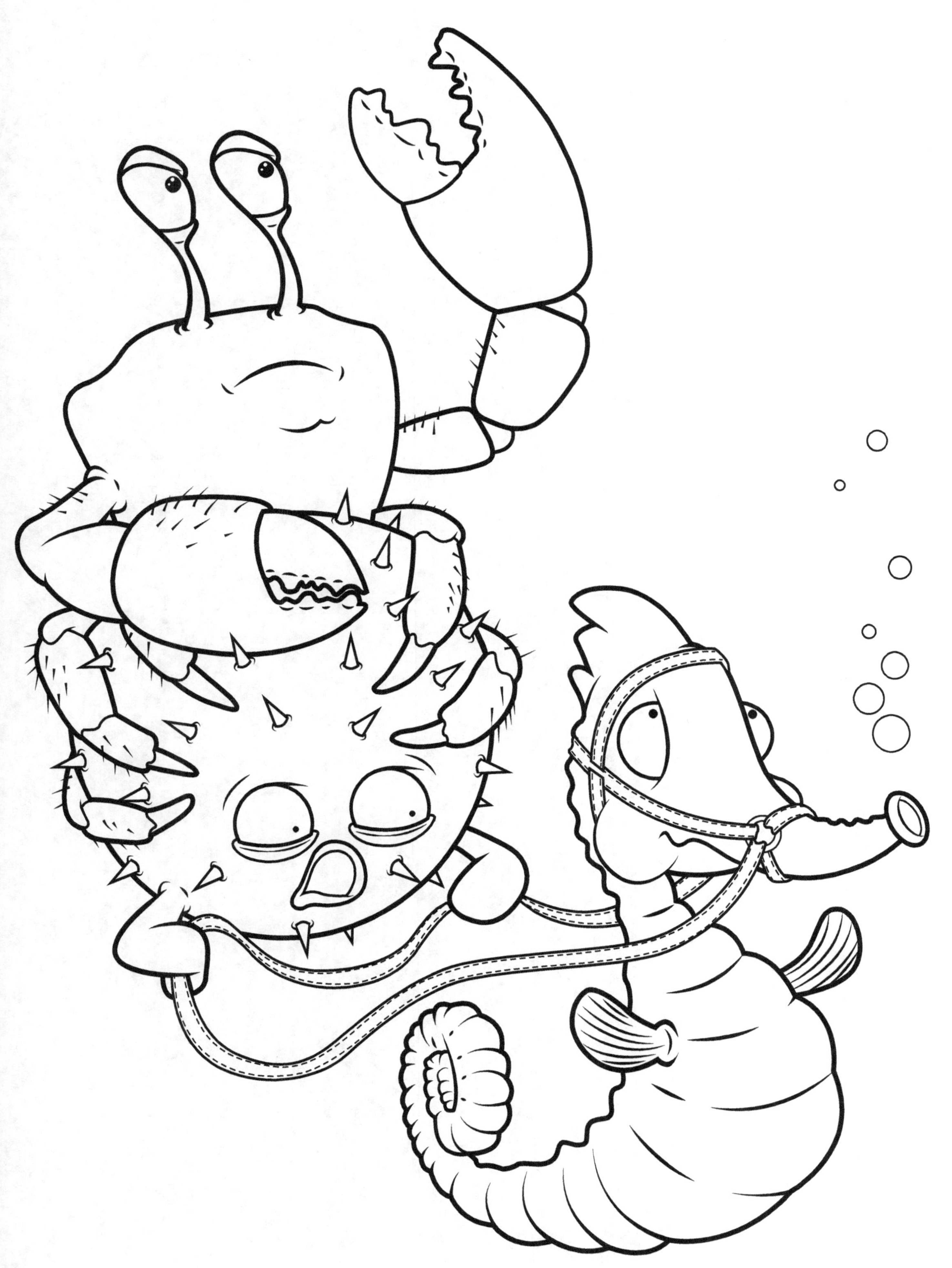

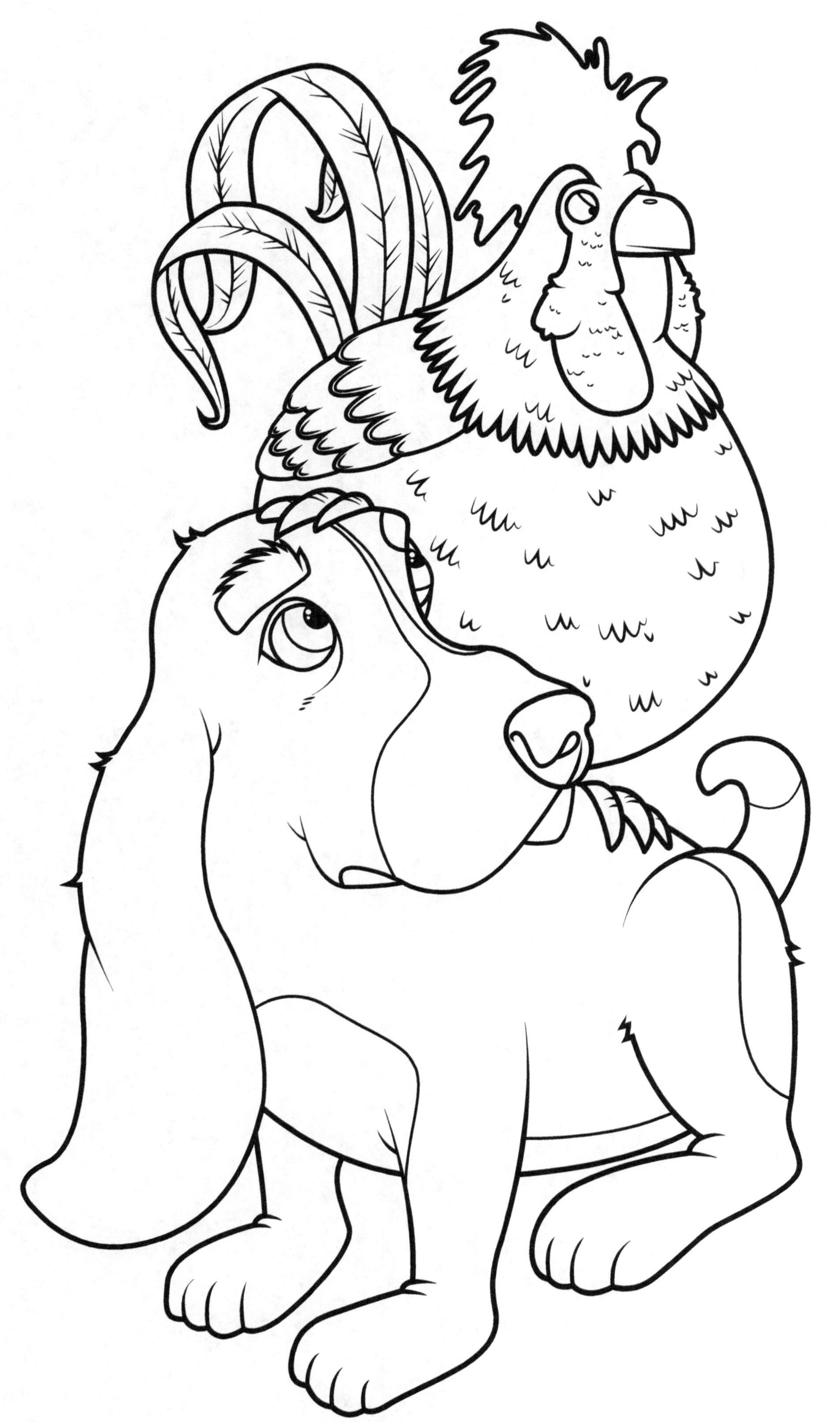

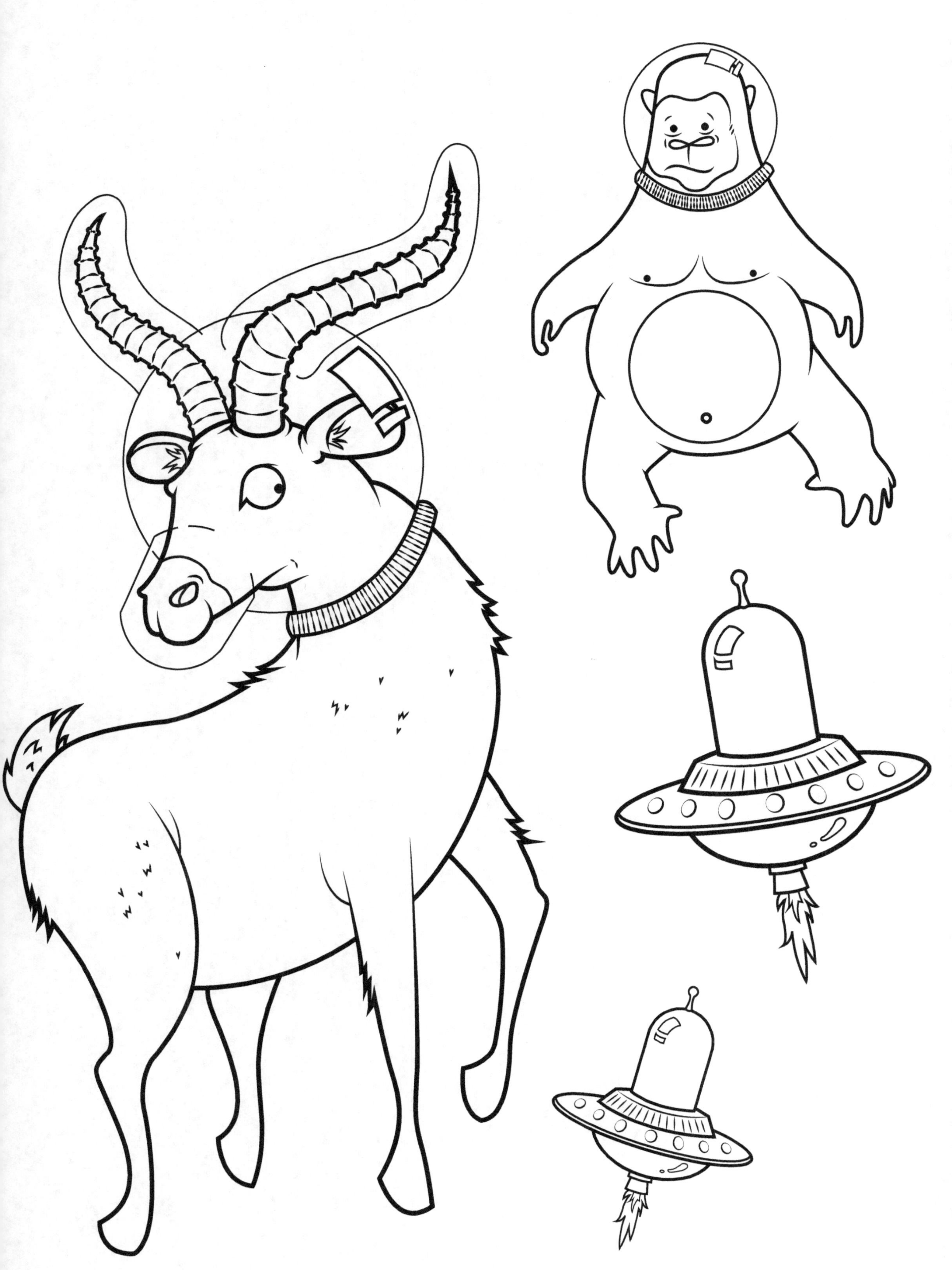

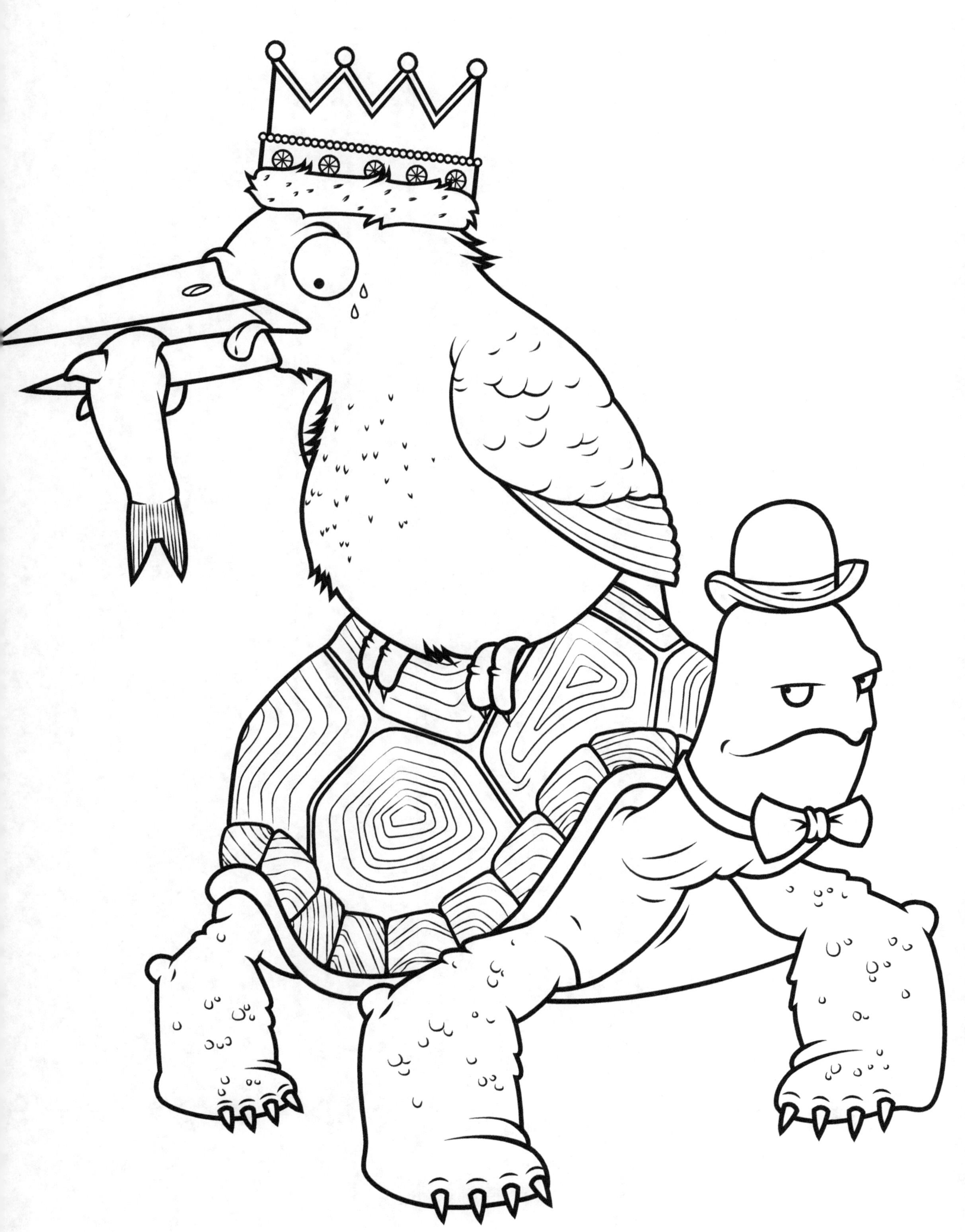

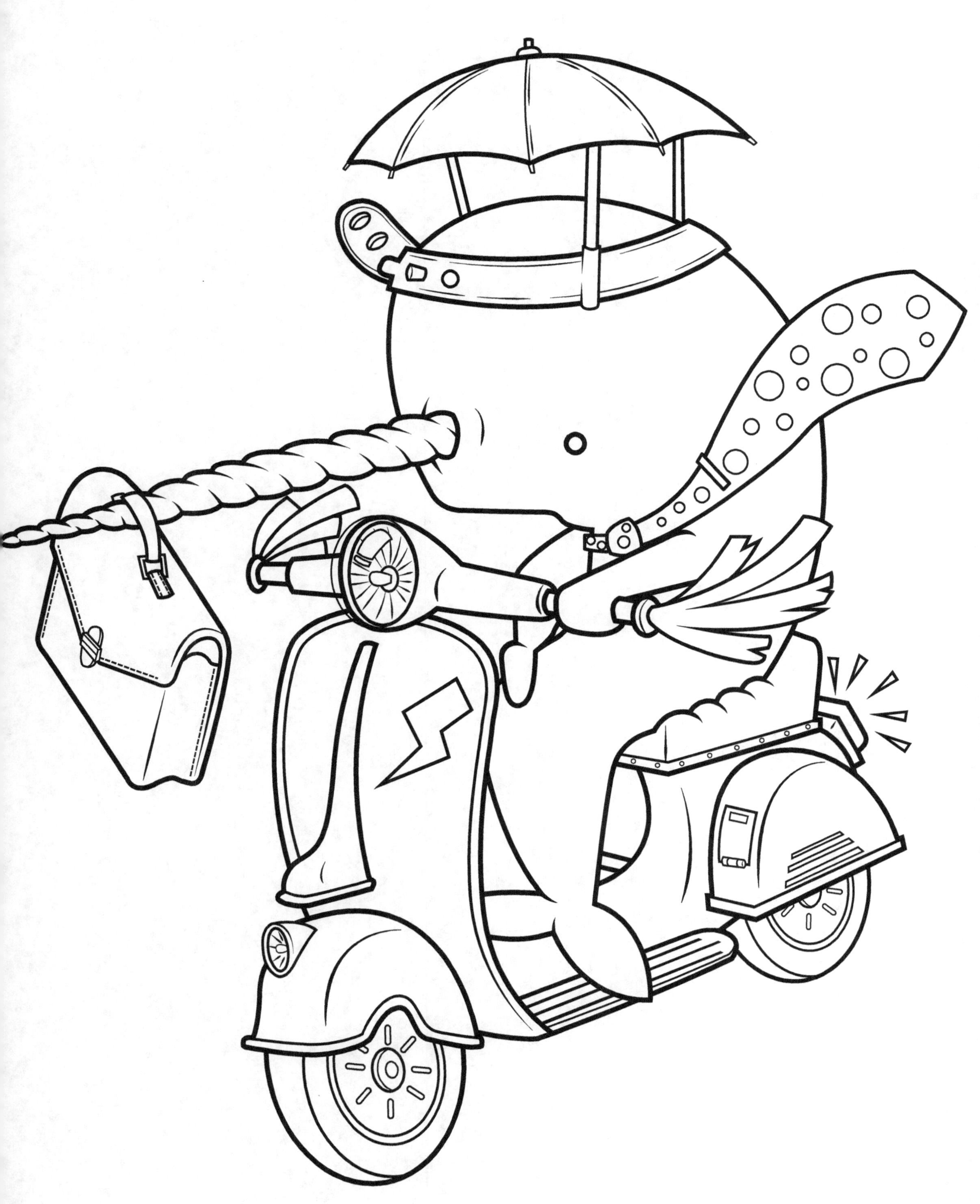

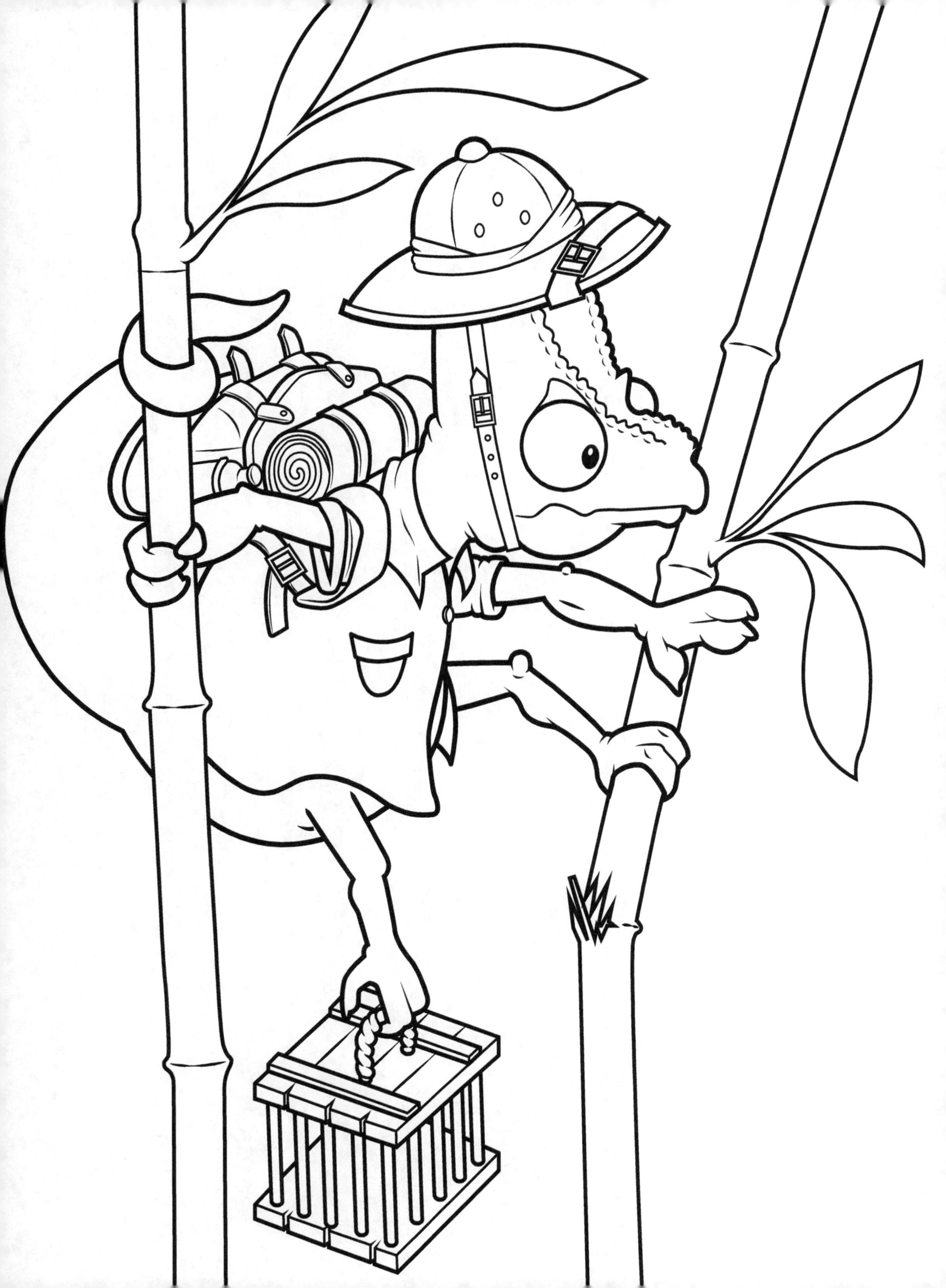

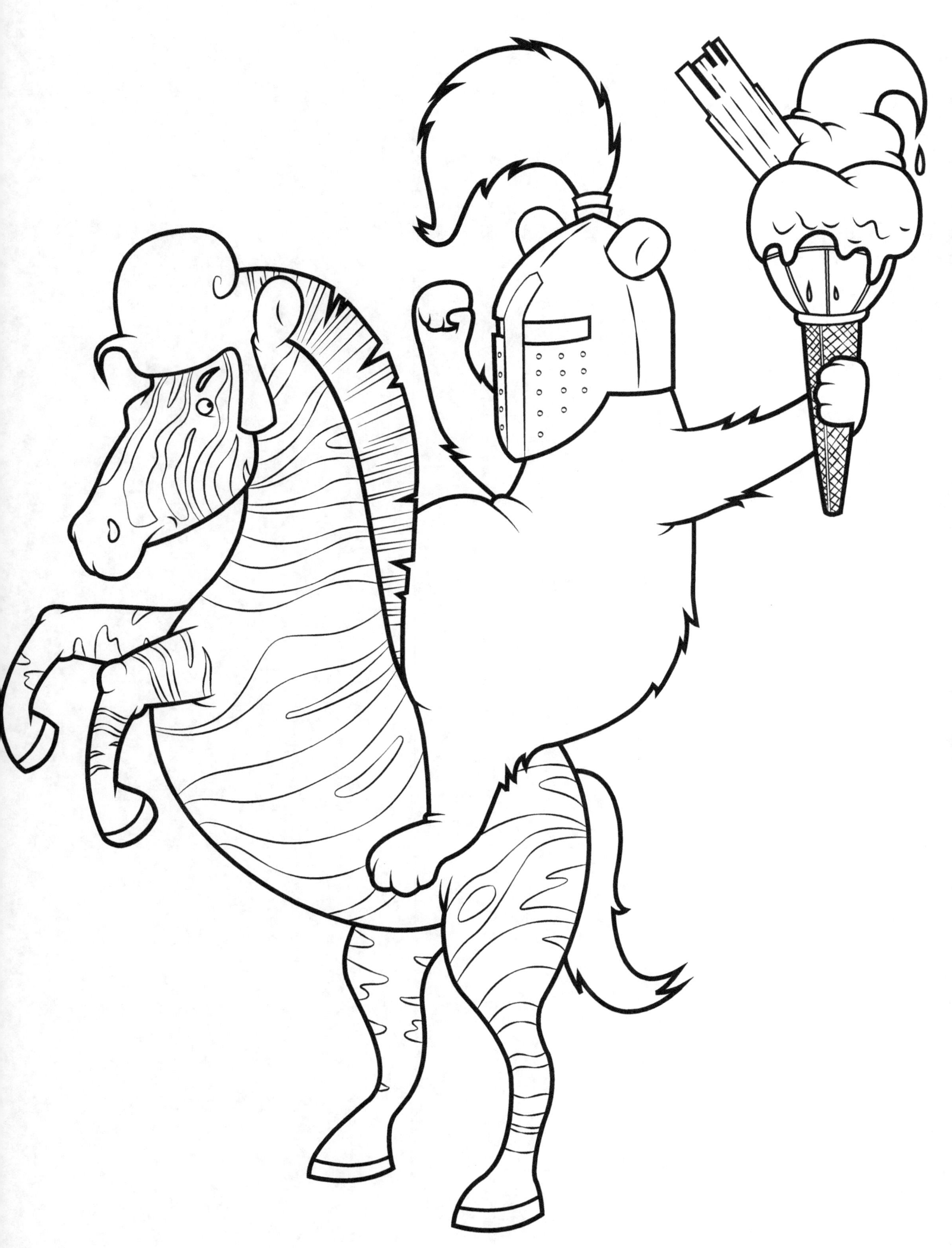

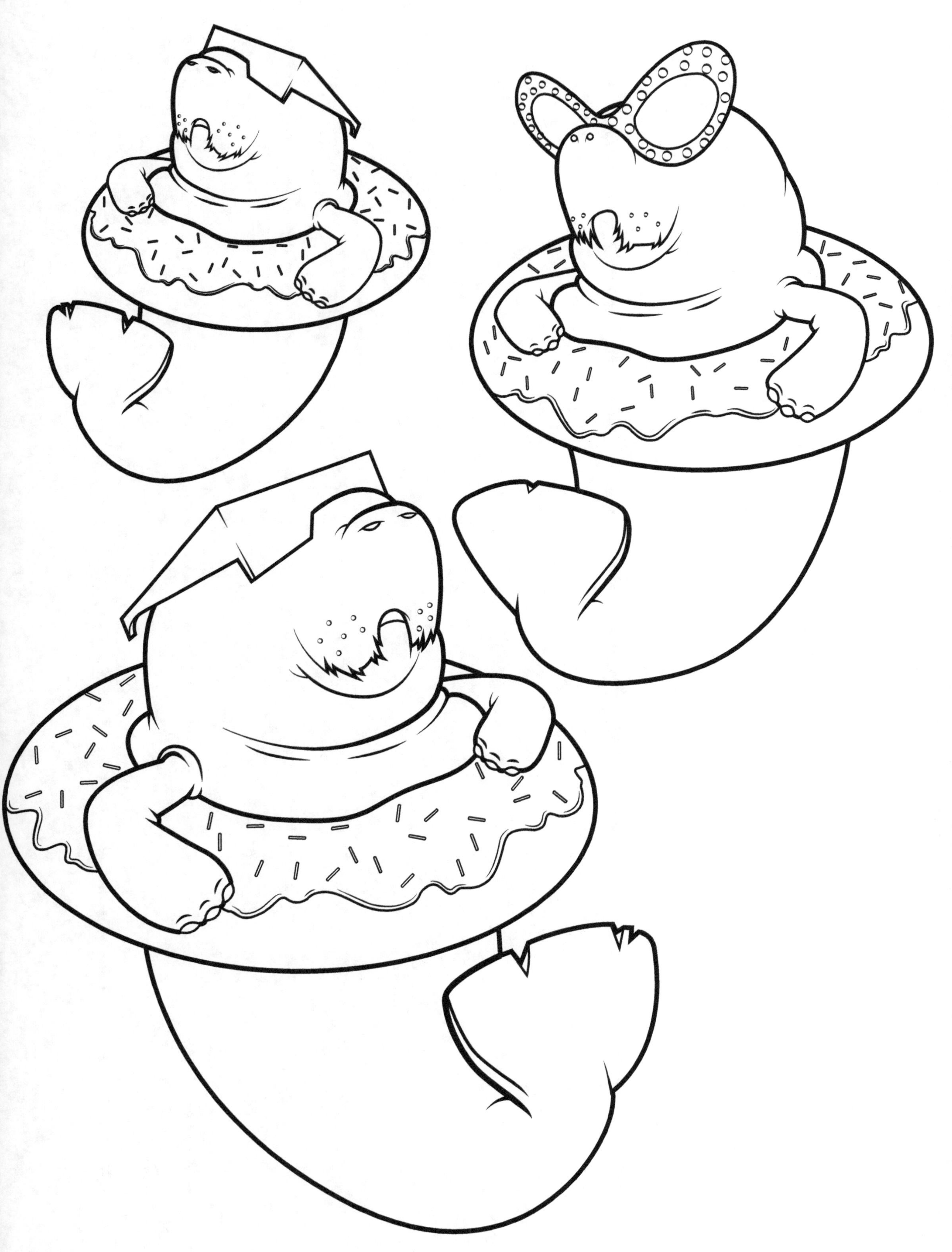

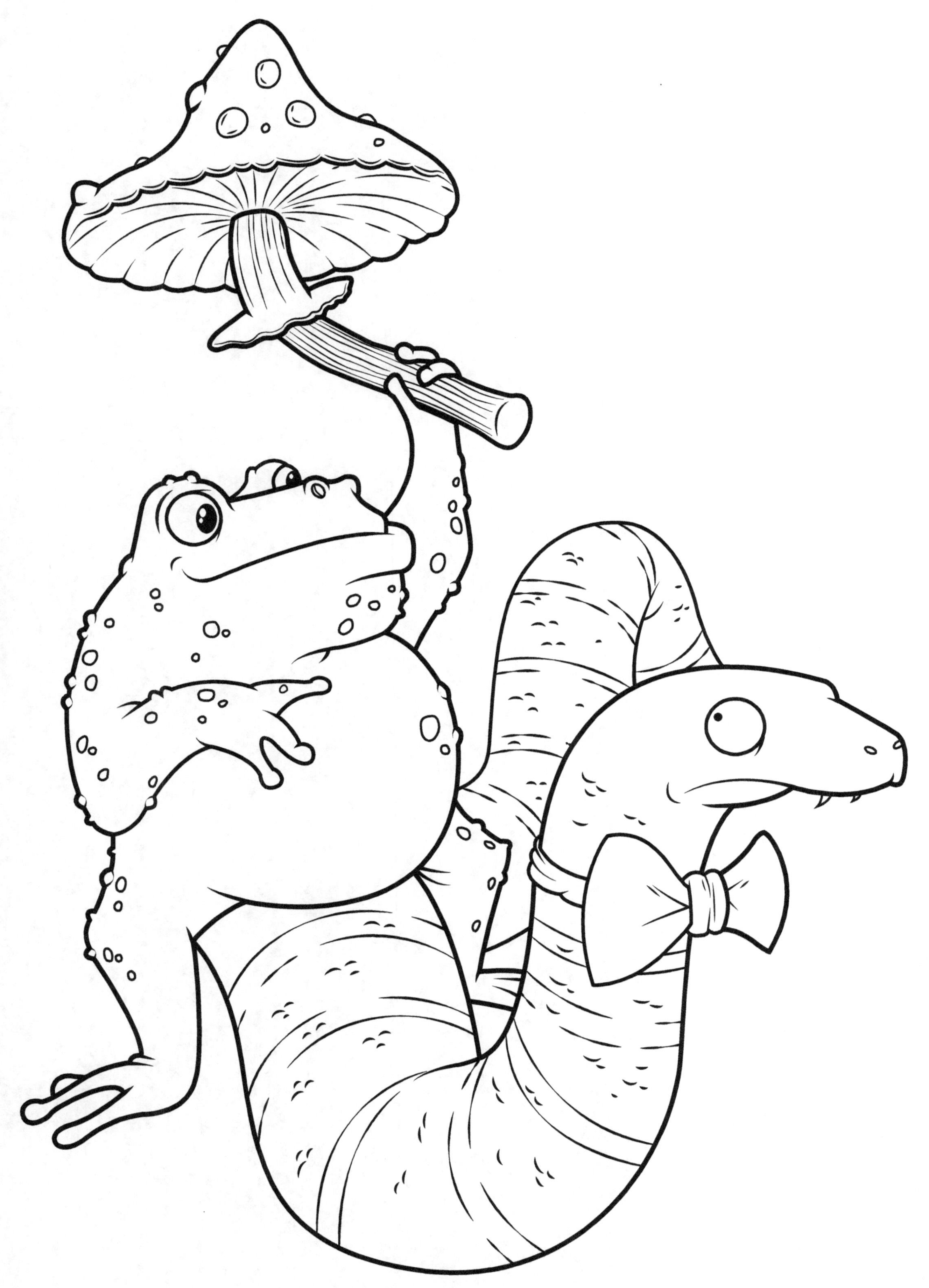

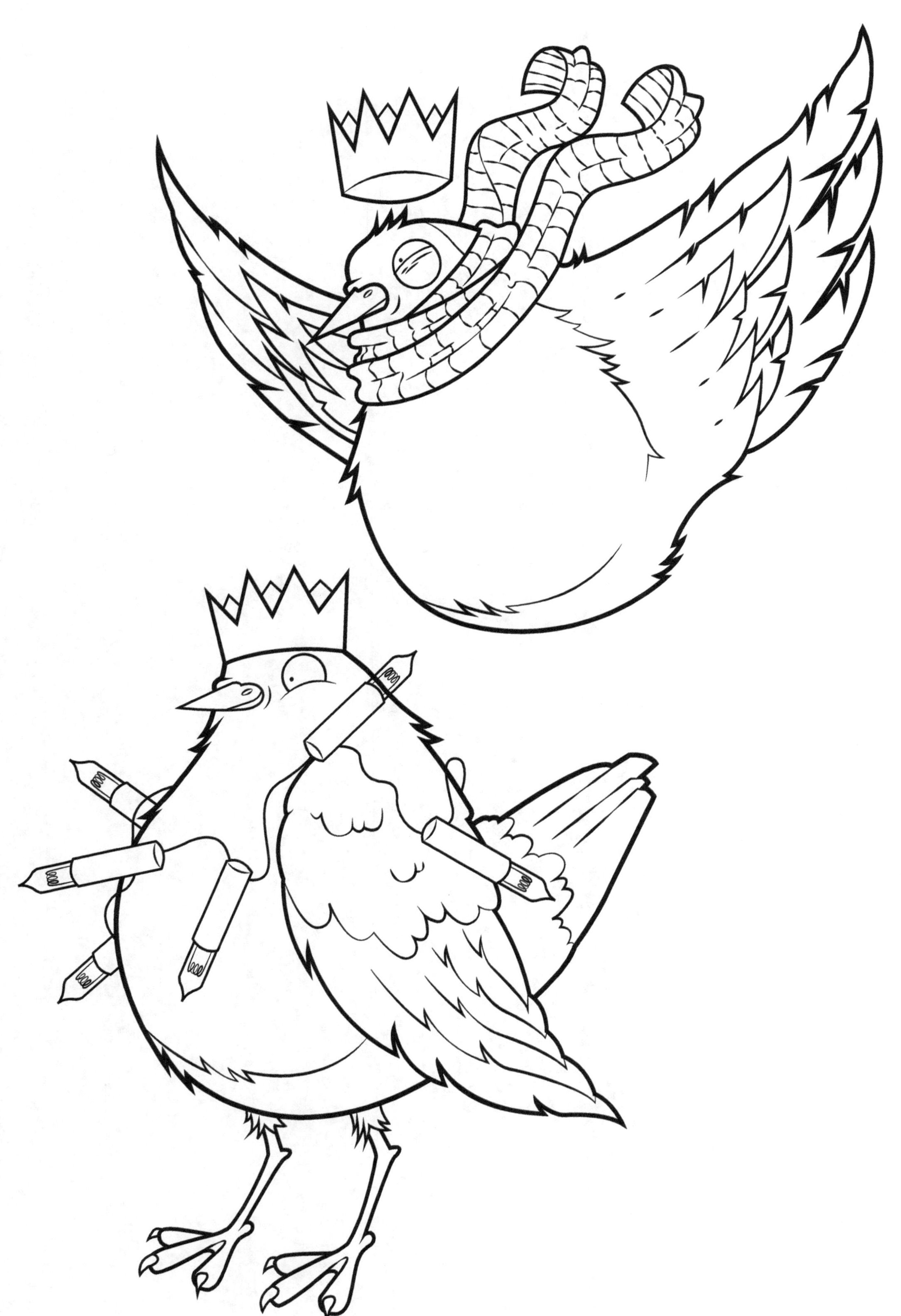

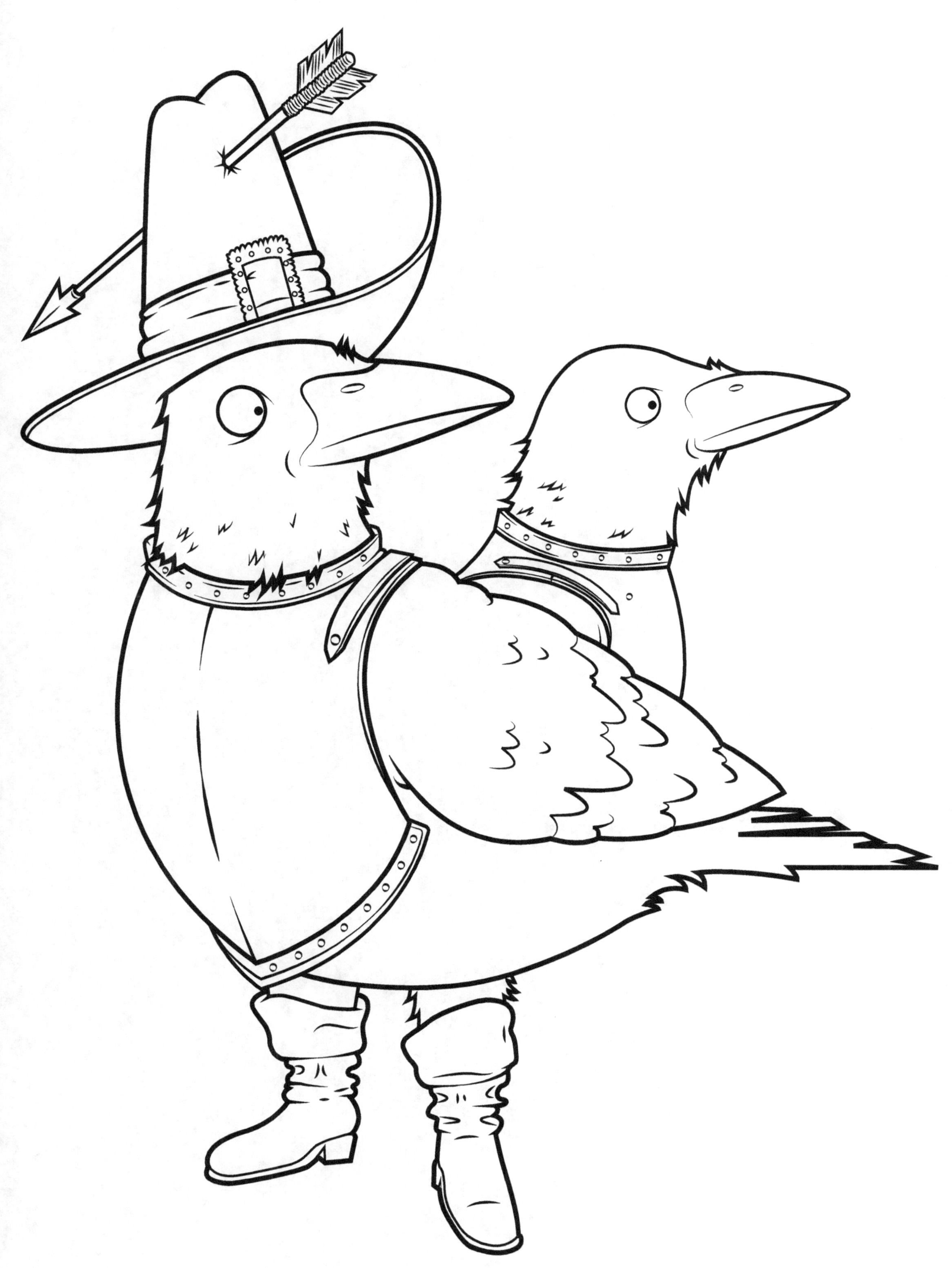

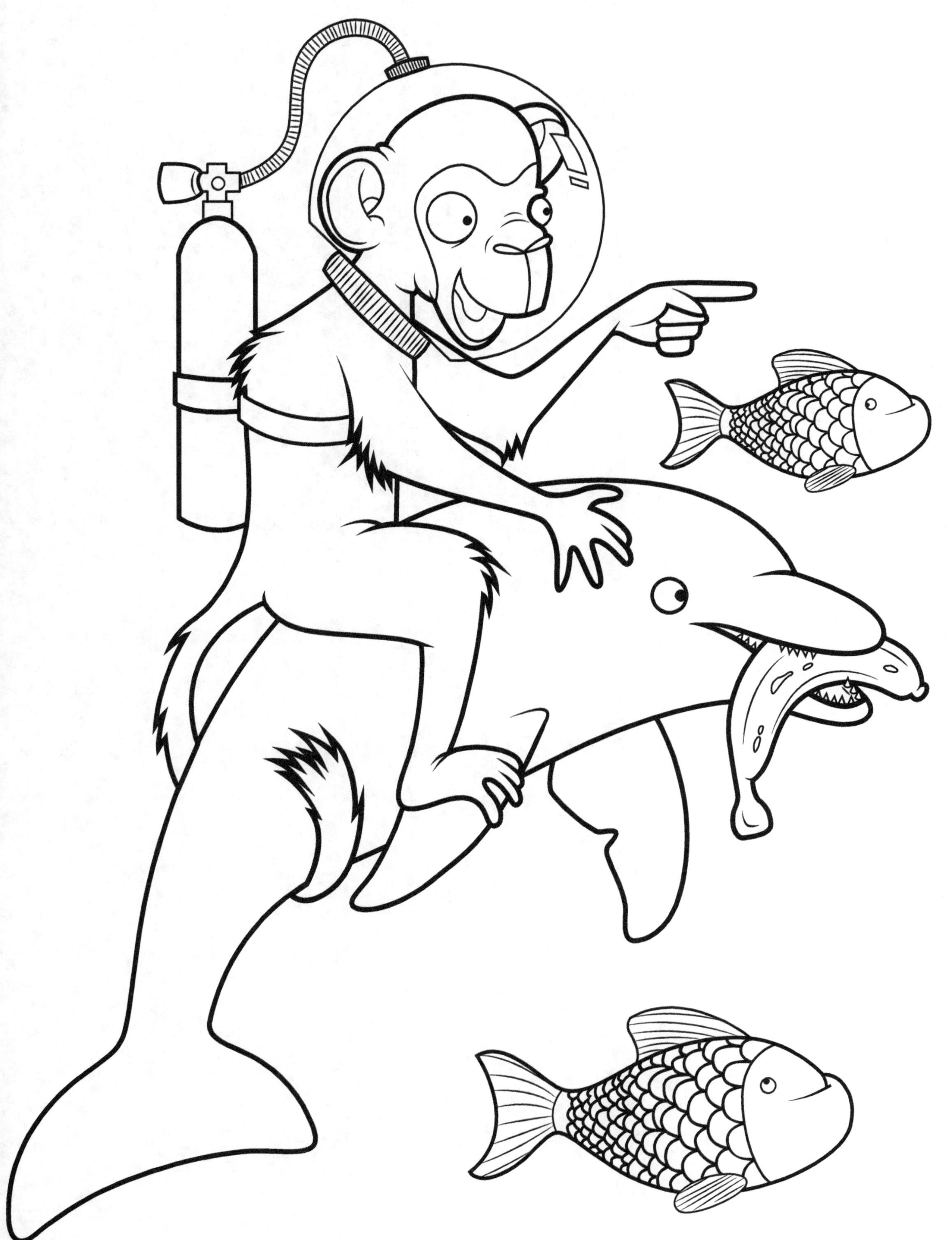

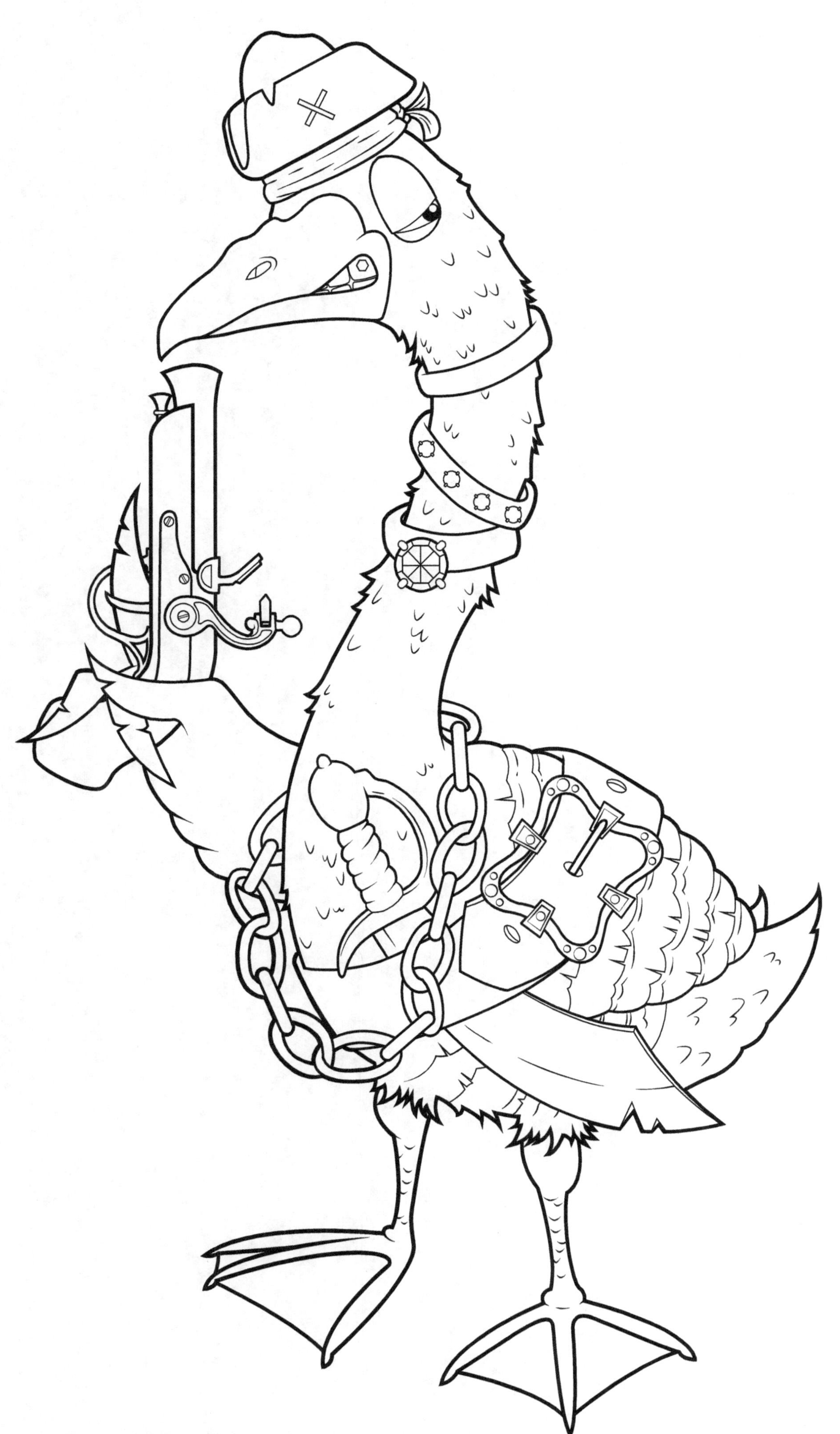

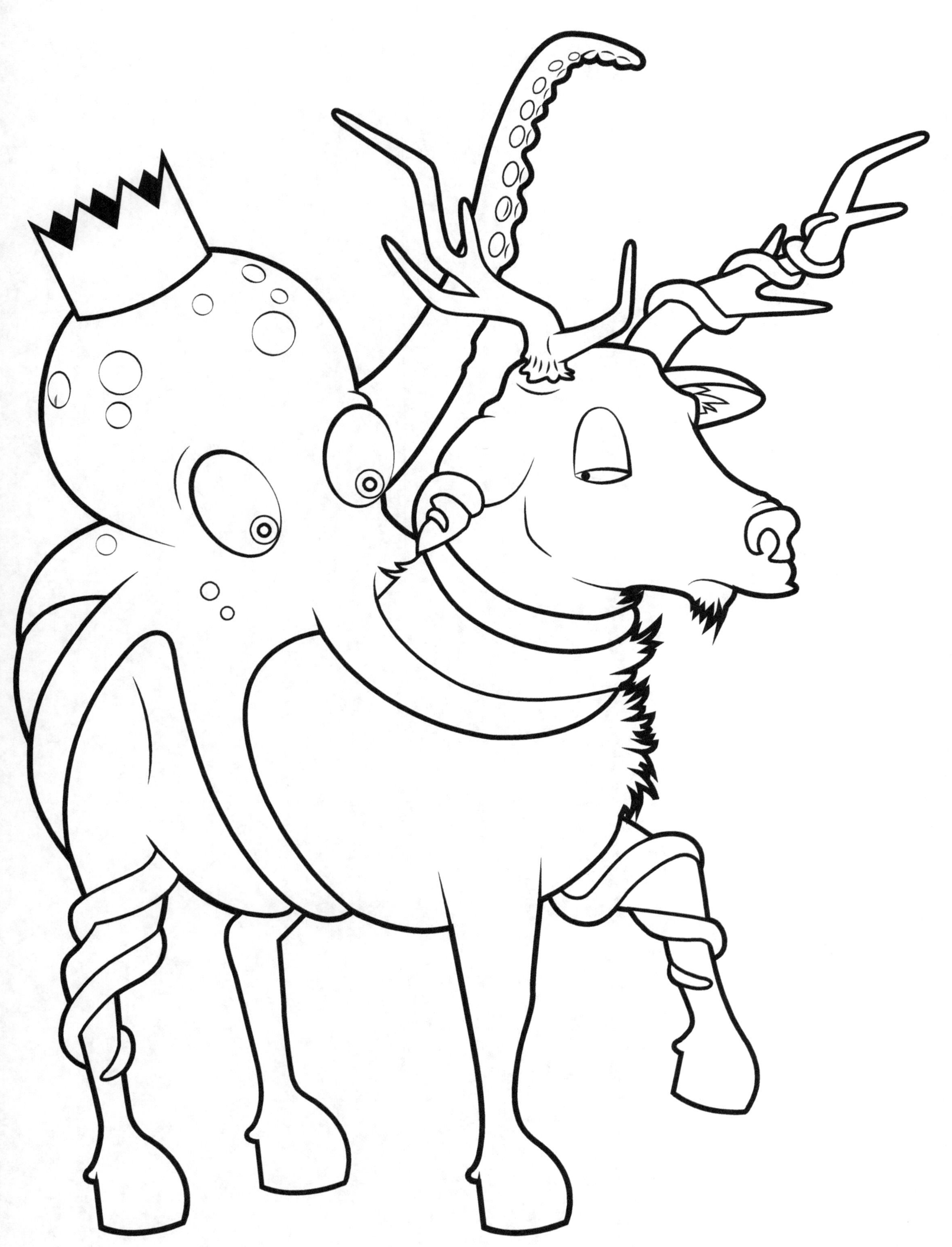

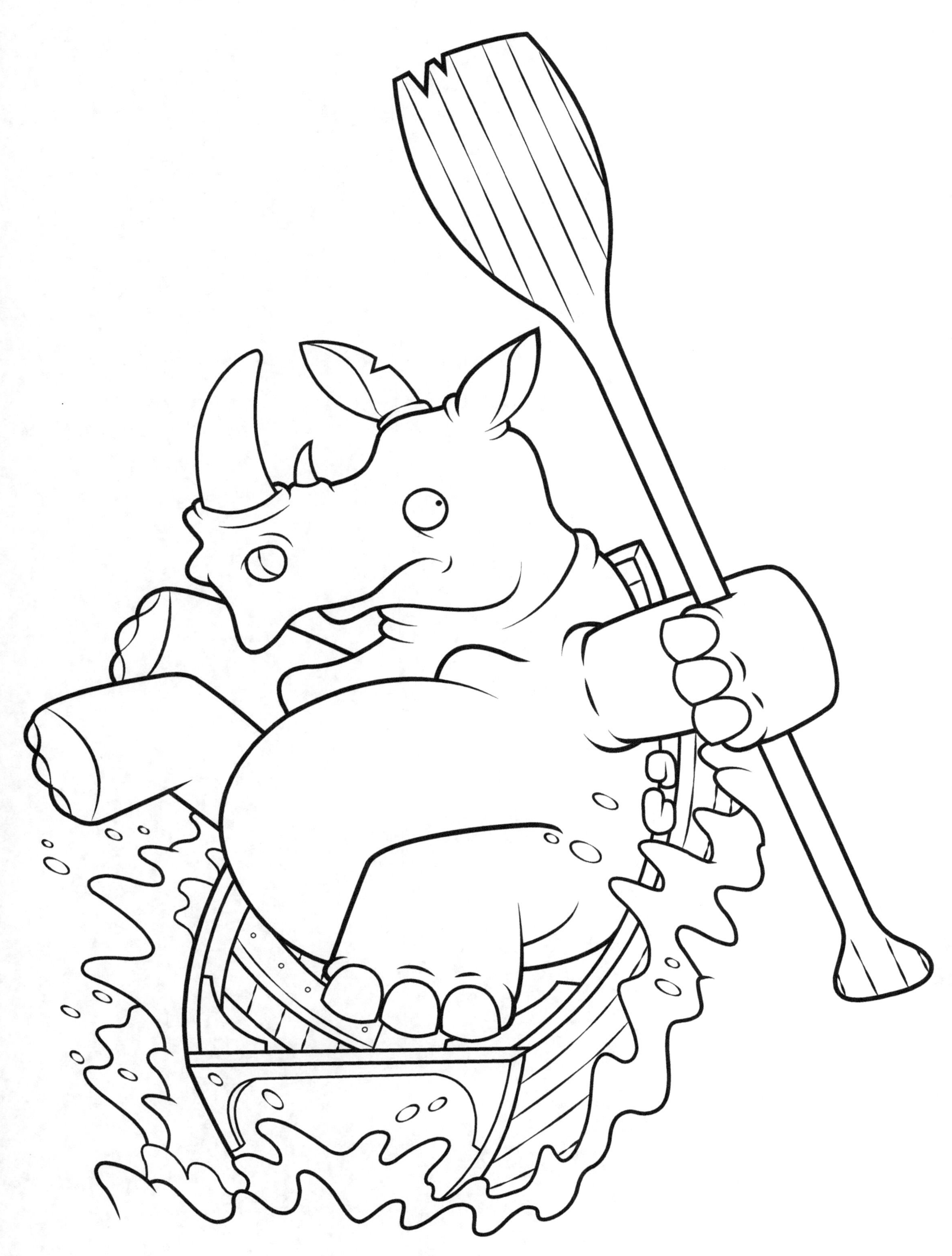

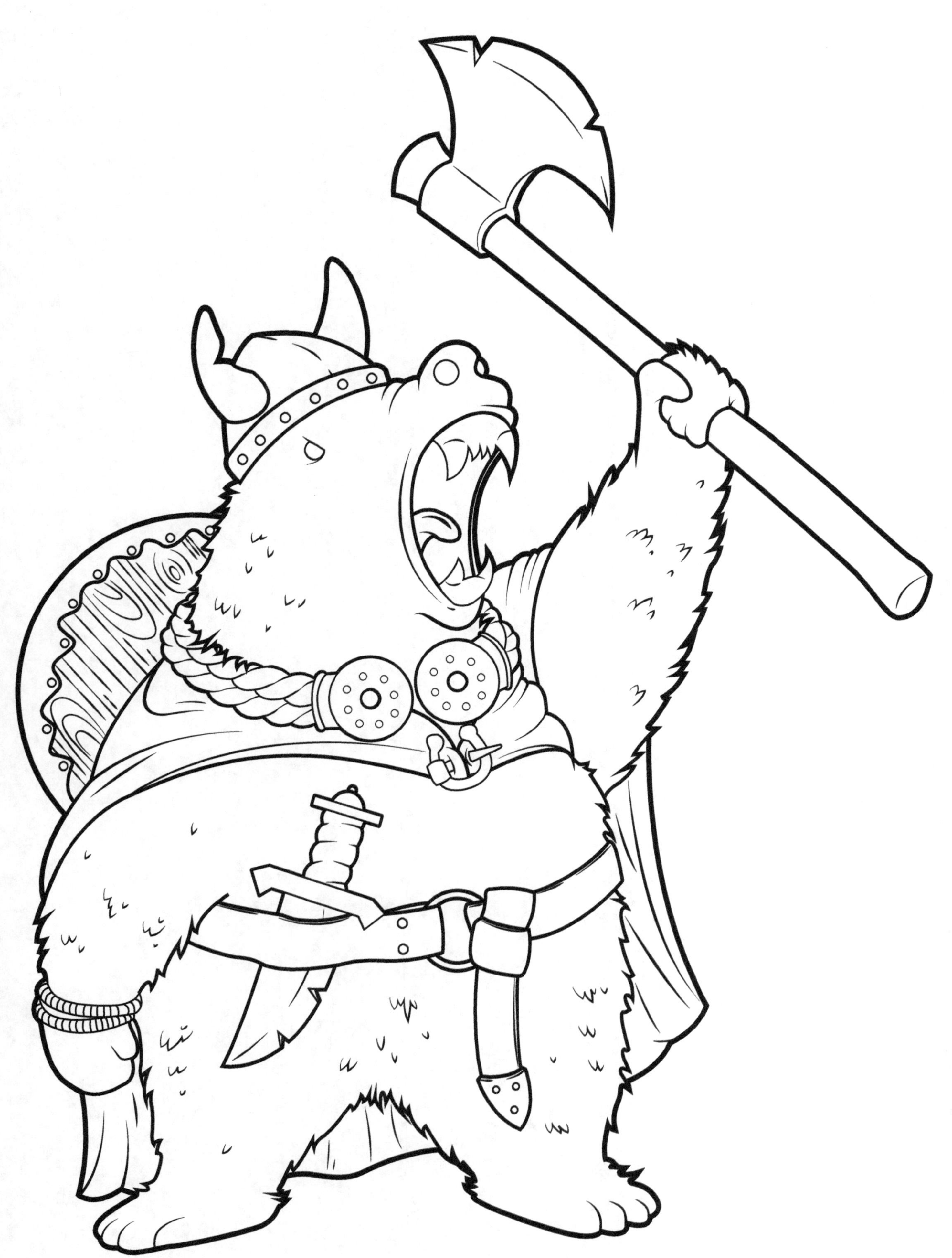

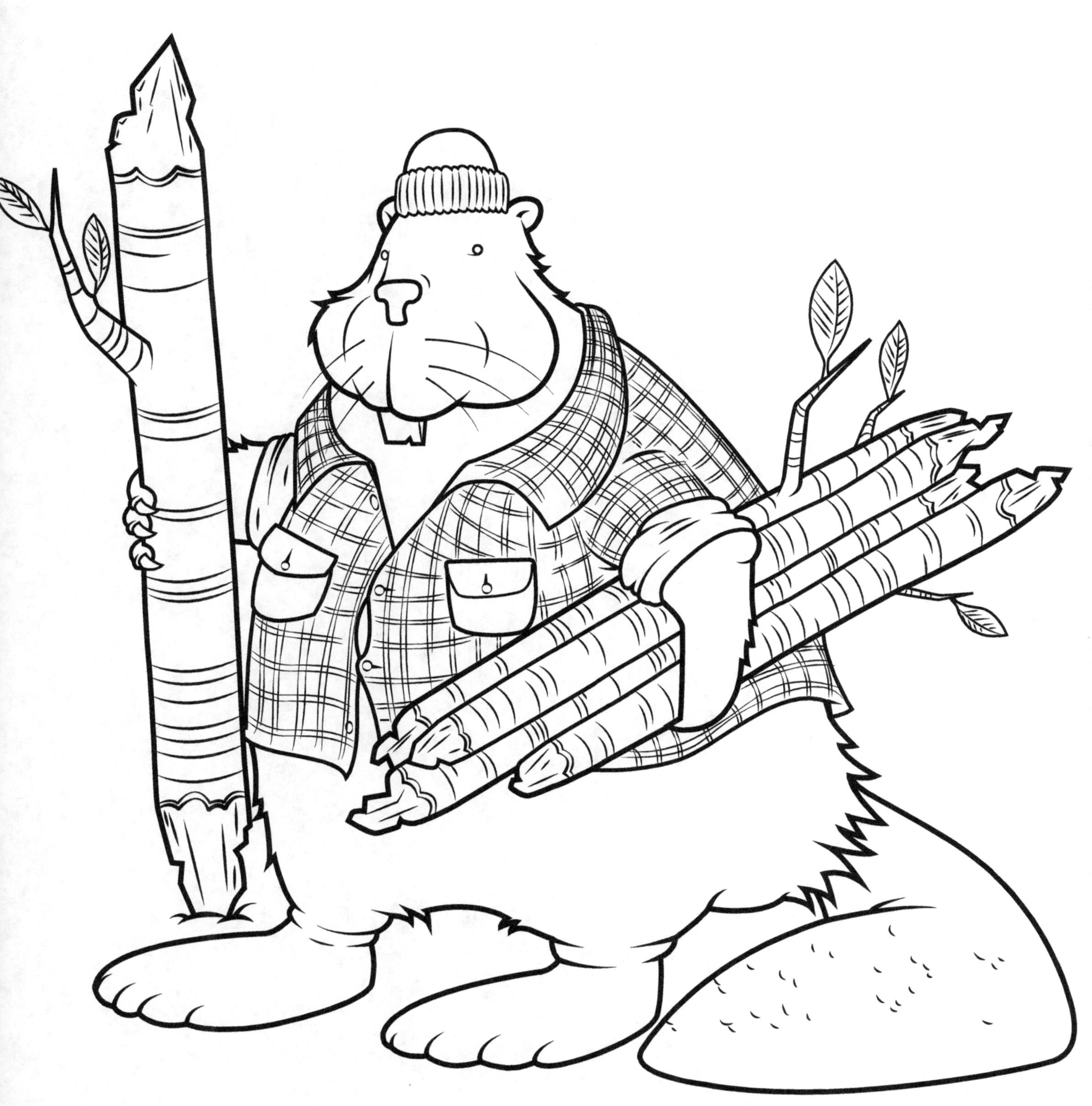

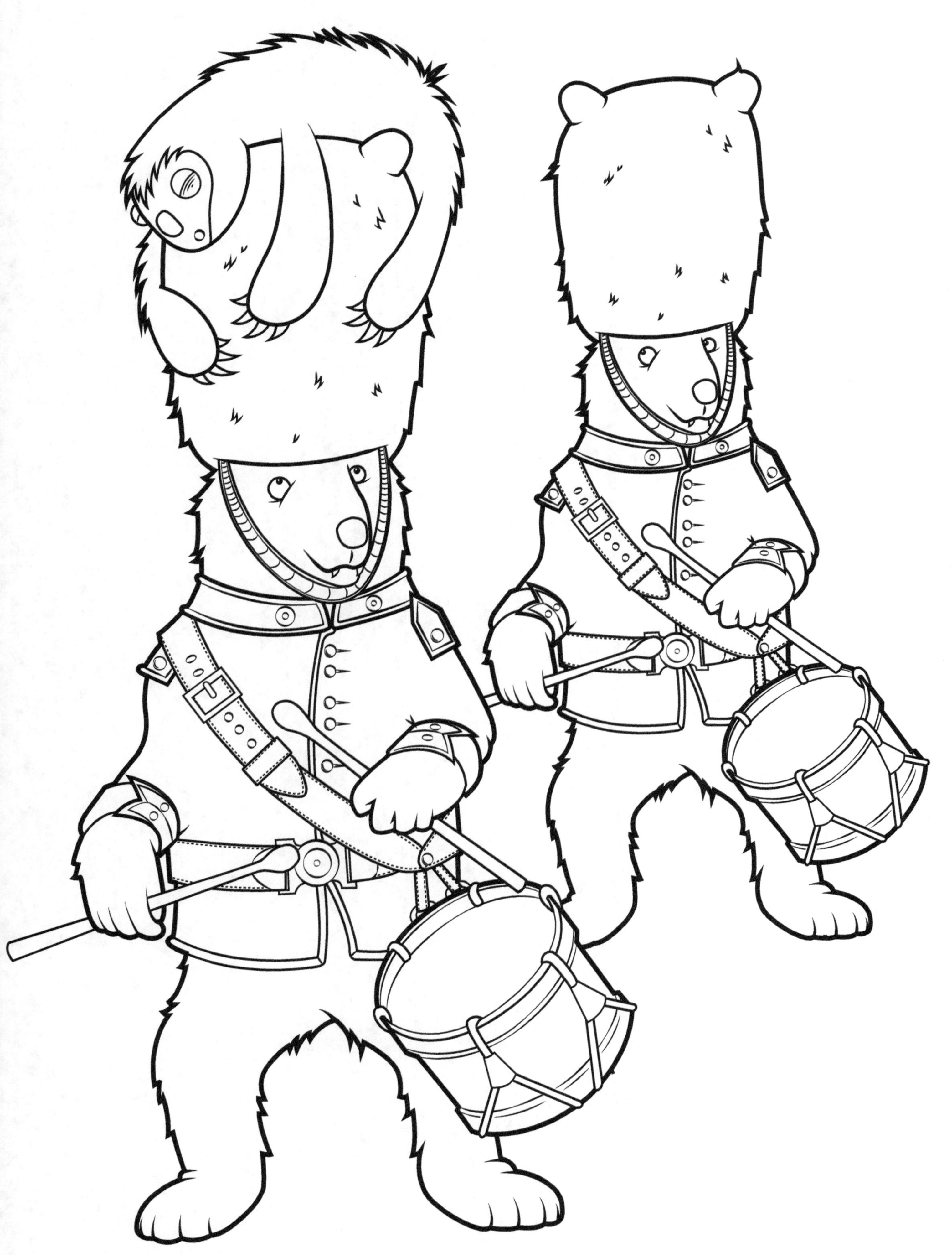

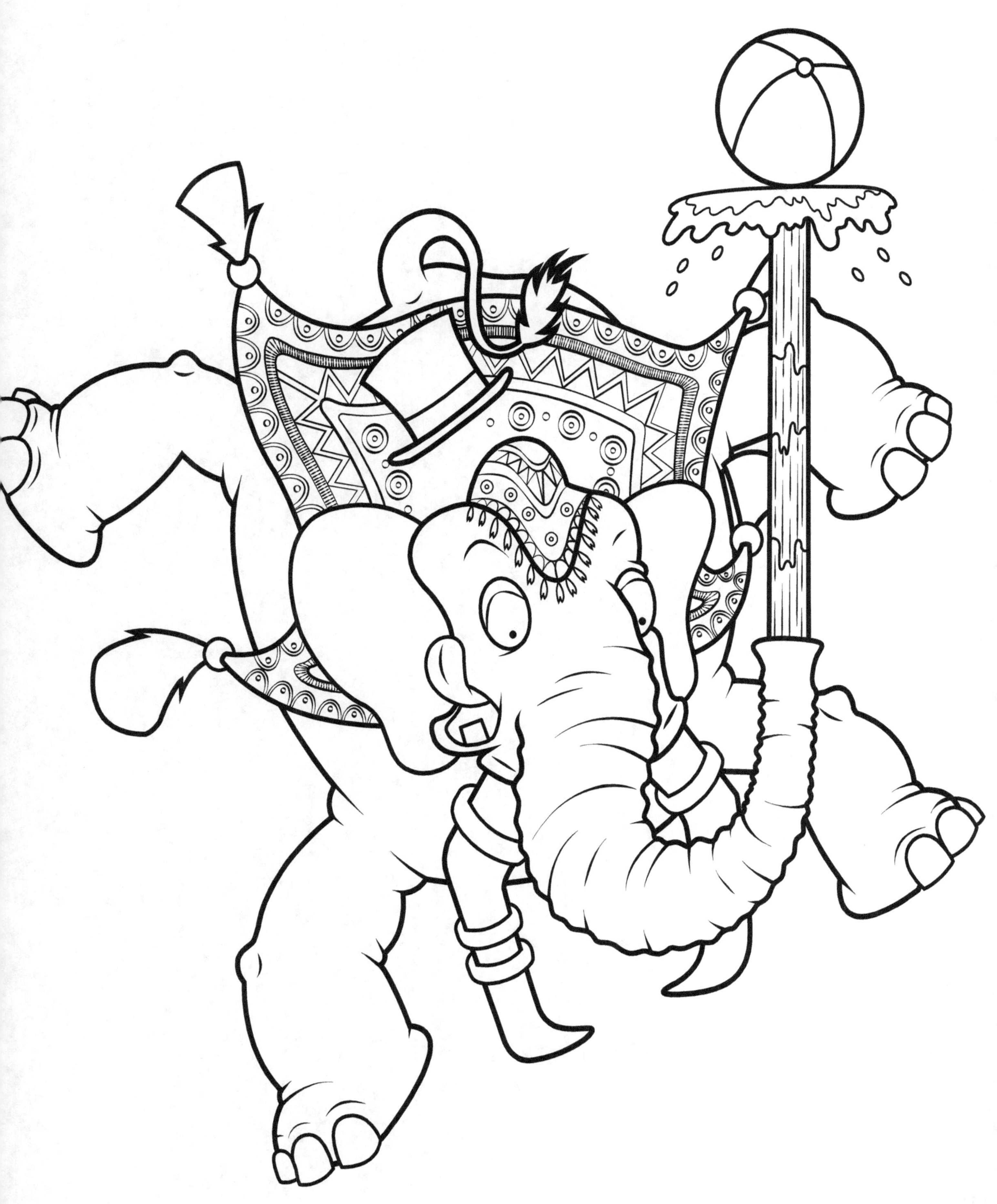